Jessica Finnis

OXFORD
UNIVERSITY PRESS

1

Our new things

Vocabulary Presentation

1 Listen, point and repeat. 01

string

tape

dictionary

paint brushes

easel

whiteboard

sink

rubber bands

globe

paint pots

2 Listen and read. 02

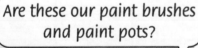

Are these our paint brushes and paint pots?

Yes, they are.

Is this your globe?

Yes, it is.

Oh no. Penny, is that your dictionary?

No it isn't. It's his dictionary.

Sorry.

It's OK.

Put it in the sink, please Jess.

3 Listen again and repeat. Act.

Go to page 34

1 Look and say.

Let's learn!

Is this your new whiteboard?
Yes, it is.

Are these our paint brushes?
Yes, they are.

Are those his paint pots?
No, they aren't.

We use *is* with **that** and **this**. We use *are* with **these** and **those**.

2 Write. Use *Is* or *Are*.

① ___Is___ this your globe?

② _____ these your rubber bands?

③ _____ that your tape?

④ _____ those your paint brushes?

3 Talk! Look at things in the classroom. Point, ask and answer.

Is that a whiteboard?

No, it isn't.

Are these your rubber bands?

Yes, they are.

Go to **35**

They're happy now!

Vocabulary Presentation

1 Listen, point and repeat. 03

bored

excited

funny

embarrassed

comfortable

warm

wet

dry

lively

full

2 Listen and read. 04

We're bored.

Let's play a game. What animal am I?

You're a very lively elephant!

He's very funny!

Are you bored now, Jess?

No ... I'm embarrassed.

3 Listen again and repeat. Act.

Go to page 36

1 Look and say.

Let's learn!

I'm funny.

Are you comfortable?
Yes, I am.

Is she hungry?
No, she isn't. She's full.

Opposites: hungry – full   wet – dry   bored – excited   tired – lively

2 Write.

I'm   ~~She's~~   Are   It's

1   <u>She's</u> wet.

2   _____ dry.

3   _____ you bored?

4   _____ funny.

3 **Talk!** Act. Ask and answer.

bored   excited   embarrassed   comfortable   warm   lively   full

Are you full?   Yes, I am.

Are you excited?   No, I'm not.

Go to page 37

Vocabulary Presentation

1 Listen, point and repeat. 05

under

on top of

opposite

ice skate

have a race

make a den

throw snowballs

climb a mountain

build a sandcastle

cross the road

2 Listen and read. 06

That's my penfriend, Maria.

Oh. Can you ice skate?

No, I can't ice skate.

They can build sandcastles quite well.

Look, a cool den.

She's on top of a mountain!

Can you run, Jess?

Yes, I can run very well!

OK. Let's have a race after lunch.

3 Listen again and repeat. Act.

Go to page 38

1 Look and say.

Let's learn!

I can make a den **very well.**

Can you cross the road? Yes, I can.

Sam can ice skate **very well.** Toby can ice skate **quite well.**

very well ✔✔   quite well ✔

2 Circle the correct words.

1 They can cross the road **very** / **quite** well.

2 I can ice skate **very** / **quite** well.

3 They **can** / **can't** make a den.

4 He **can't** / **can** climb a mountain very well.

3 Talk! Ask and answer. Use *quite* and *very*.

| ice skate | climb | cross | build | make | throw | play | do |

Can you ice skate?

Yes, I can ice skate quite well.

Can you build a sandcastle?

No, I can't.

Go to page 39

Have you got a milkshake?

Vocabulary Presentation

1 Listen, point and repeat. 07

 prunes

 picnic blanket

 pineapple

 popcorn

 pie

 strawberries

 raspberries

 blackberries

 flask

 basket

2 Listen and read. 08

Yum! Look, they've got strawberries, blackberries and raspberries.

Pick your own fruit
Strawberries
Blackberries
Raspberries

I've got some baskets to put the fruit in.

I'm thirsty. Have you got any water?

I've got some prune juice in this flask.

Look, he's got some pineapples!

EXIT
FARM SHOP

I haven't got any strawberries now.

3 Listen again and repeat. Act.

 Go to page 40

1 Look and say.

Let's learn!

Have you got any popcorn?

I haven't got any pie.

They've got some strawberries.

We use **some** with positive sentences.
We use **any** with negative sentences and questions.

2 Write. Use *some* or *any*.

1 You've got ___some___ blackberries.

2 I haven't got _____ prunes.

3 Have you got _____ pineapples?

4 They've got _____ baskets.

5 Have you got _____ raspberries?

6 We haven't got _____ strawberries.

3 **Talk!** Choose five items from Exercise 1, page 8. Ask and answer.

Have you got any strawberries?

No, I haven't. Have you got any prunes?

Yes, I have.

Go to page **41**

I've got some … They haven't got any … Have you got any … ? Unit 4 9

Vocabulary Presentation

1 Listen, point and repeat. 09

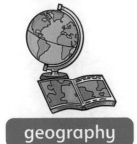
geography

science lab

head teacher

school bus

entrance

history

woodwork

canteen

school gate

workshop

2 Listen and read. 10

When have you got science?

After lunch. What have you got?

I'm not sure.

We've got lunch now in the canteen.

Then we've got woodwork.

Hmmm. Where have we got woodwork?

Here's the workshop and there's our classroom.

And here's the head teacher's office!

3 Listen again and repeat. Act.

Go to page 42

1 Look and say.

Let's learn!

Where have we got history?
We've got history in our classroom.

What have you got now?
I've got geography.

When have you got science?
I've got science on Thursday.

Use **where** for location, **what** for the subject and **when** for time.

2 Write.

Where   What   When

Where have we got science?

_____ have you got geography?

_____ have we got after lunch?

3 **Talk!** Use *what, when* and *where* to talk about school this week

What have we got after lunch?

We've got maths.

Where have we got PE tomorrow?

In the playground.

Go to page 43

Let's play after school!

Vocabulary Presentation

1 Listen, point and repeat. 🔊 11

go camping

paint a picture

watch a DVD

do sports

go to the park

play the drums

go for a walk

do homework

go to a café

visit friends

2 Listen and read. 🔊 12

3 Listen again and repeat. Act.

Go to page 44

1 Look and say.

Let's learn!

What do you do after school?
I go to the park.

Do you go to a café every Saturday?
Yes, I do.

2 Write.

| Do you | I do sports. | ~~What do you~~ | No, I don't. |

① __What do you__ do every Thursday?
I watch DVDs.

② _____ visit friends after school?
Yes, I do.

③ What do you do every Friday?
_____

④ Do you go for a walk every Sunday?
_____

3 Talk! Write activities. Ask and answer.

Monday	Tuesday	Wednesday	Thursday	Friday
do sports	_____	_____	_____	_____

What do you every Monday?

I do sports. Do you do sports on Monday?

No, I don't.

Go to page 45

What do you do after school? Do you ...? **Unit 6**   13

Let's buy presents!

Vocabulary Presentation

1 Listen, point and repeat. 🔊 13

bouncy castle

party bag

clown

party games

jelly

ribbon

bow

wrapping paper

paper plate

napkins

2 Listen and read. 🔊 14

3 Listen again and repeat. Act.

Go to page 46

1 Look and say.

Let's learn!

What do you like **to play** at parties?
I like **to play** party games.

What do you like **to eat** at parties?
I like **to eat** jelly from a paper plate!

What do you like **to wear** at parties?
I like **to wear** my party dress.

2 Circle the correct words.

1 What do you like to **to do** / do / **does** at parties?

2 What do you like **to wear** / **wear** / **wears** every weekend?

3 What does he like to **eats** / **to eat** / **eat** for breakfast?

4 What do they like **watch** / **watches** / **to watch** on TV?

3 Talk! Ask and answer.

to watch	to play	to do	to wear	to eat	to drink

What do you like to wear after school?   I like to wear my T-shirt.

What do you like to eat for lunch?   I like to eat pizza.

Go to page **47**

Vocabulary Presentation

1 Listen, point and repeat. 15

wake up

wash my hair

wash my hands

have a shower

have a dream

brush my teeth

get dressed

go downstairs

go upstairs

go to sleep

2 Listen and read. 16

What time do you go to sleep?

I go to sleep at 8 o'clock.

What time do you wake up?

I wake up at 7 o'clock.

Please have a shower and brush your teeth.

What's the time?

Bedtime!

Toby, go to your bed.

We're scared. Sam has bad dreams and I don't like the dark.

Oh, boys! Goodnight.

3 Listen again and repeat. Act.

Go to page 48

1 Look and say.

Let's learn!

What time **do** you get dressed in the morning?

I get dressed **at** 8 o'clock.

What time **does** he have a shower?

He has a shower **at** 8 o'clock.

2 Write. Use *do* or *does*.

1 What time ___does___ your mum wake up?

2 What time _____ she brush her teeth?

3 What time _____ they go to sleep?

4 What time _____ he get dressed in the morning?

5 What time _____ you have a shower?

6 What time _____ she wash her hair?

3 **Talk!** **Ask and answer.**

| wake up | have a shower | go upstairs to bed |
| go to sleep | go to school | do your homework |

What time do you get up?

I get up at 6 o'clock.

What time do you go to sleep?

I go to sleep at 8 o'clock.

Go to page 49

Where does she work?

Vocabulary Presentation

1 Listen, point and repeat. 🎵 17

university

market

campsite

office block

petrol station

post office

art gallery

aquarium

pet shop

ticket office

2 Listen and read. 🎵 18

Where do your mum and dad work?

Dad works at the university and Mum works in an art gallery.

What time do they start work in the morning?

They start work at 9 o'clock.

My mum works in a pet shop.

I want to work in a post office.

I want to work in an aquarium. I love fish! Pop pop.

3 Listen again and repeat. Act.

Go to page 50

1 Look and say.

Where do they work?
They work in an office block.

What time do you start work?
I start work at 9 o'clock

Do you like your job?
Yes, I do. I like to work at the market

2 Write.

What time does	Where does	Where do	~~What time do~~

1 _What time do_____ they start work?

2 _____ they work?

3 _____ he work?

4 _____ he start work?

3 **Talk!** Choose a place from Exercise 1, page 18. Pretend you work there. Ask and answer.

Where do you work?

I work at the university.

What time do you start work?

I start work at 8 o'clock.

Go to page 51

Vocabulary Presentation

1 Listen, point and repeat. 🔊 19

cloudy

foggy

hailing

stay inside

wear a sun hat

go on a boat

eat an ice cream

use an umbrella

wear sunglasses

ride a sled

2 Listen and read. 🔊 20

Let's go on a boat.

It's cloudy and foggy, so let's go for a walk first.

Good idea.

Later

OUCH!

Oh no, is it hailing? Let's use the umbrellas.

Quickly, Mum!

It's ice, so let's eat ice cream!

Jess, you can't eat the ice!

3 Listen again and repeat. Act.

Go to page 52

1 Look and say.

Let's learn!

It's sunny today, **so let s** wear sun hats.

Is it raining today?
Yes, it is, **so let's** stay inside.

Use **so** to connect sentences.

2 Write.

It's raining,
so let's _use_
umbrellas .
(use)

It's sunny,
so let's _____
_____ .
(wear)

It's hailing today,
so let's _____
_____ .
(stay)

It's snowing today,
so let's _____
_____ .
(ride)

3 Talk! Point and make sentences.

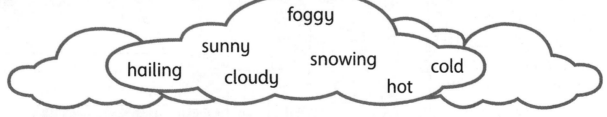

foggy
sunny
hailing   snowing   cold
cloudy   hot

It's cold, so let's put on our coats.   It's snowing, so let's throw snowballs.

It's foggy, so let's watch DVDs.

Go to page 53

Vocabulary Presentation

1 Listen, point and repeat. 21

suit

trainers

nightdress

pyjamas

earmuffs

five past

twenty past

twenty-five past

twenty-five to

ten to

2 Listen and read. 22

3 Listen again and repeat. Act.

Go to page 54

1 Look and say.

Let's learn!

Are you watching TV?
No, I'm watching DVDs.

Is Toby playing football?
Yes, he is.

What are they eating?
They're eating pizza.

Add *ing* to verbs in the present continuous.
watch = watch**ing**   eat = eat**ing**   listen = listen**ing**   play = play**ing**

2 Write.

1 Tim*'s playing* football. (play)

2 What DVDs are they _____? (watch)

3 Are you _____ to music? (listen)

4 I _____ a book. (read)

3 Talk! Point, ask and answer.

What's he eating?

He's eating cake. What's he reading?

He's reading a book.

Go to page 55

Vocabulary Presentation

1 Listen, point and repeat. 🔊 23

make a DVD

groom

bridesmaids

wedding dress

video camera

wedding ring

celebrate

decorate the cake

look in the mirror

make a speech

2 Listen and read. 🔊 24

Mum's the bride, Dad's the groom and this is the bridesmaid.

What's the bridesmaid doing?

She's helping with the wedding dress.

This man's making a DVD of the wedding. What's your grandma doing?

She's decorating the cake.

What are you doing?

We're celebrating your wedding!

3 Listen again and repeat. Act.

Go to page 56

24   Unit 12   Celebrations

1 Look and say.

Let's learn!

What **are the** bridesmaids doing? **They're** looking in the mirror.

What's **the** groom doing? **He's making** a speech.

What's **your** sister doing? **She's** listening to music.

2 Write the sentences.

 ①

The guests are eating.
They're
eating.

②

The boy's wearing a suit.
_____
_____

③

The woman's watching the wedding DVD.
_____
_____

④

The bride and groom are eating the cake.
_____
_____

3 Talk! Look at the vocabulary items on page 24. Point, ask and answer.

What's the man doing?

He's making a speech.

What's the woman doing?

She's dancing.

Go to page **57**

What's the ... doing? What are the ... doing? What's your ... doing? **Unit 12**

25

Vocabulary Presentation

1 Listen, point and repeat. 25

| barn | hen | butterfly | bee | tractor |

| corn | calf | foal | lamb | ducklings |

2 Listen and read. 26

The ducklings are noisier and funnier than the hens.

The hens are noisy!

Let's go and see the sheep.

They're called lambs.

Look! A baby sheep.

They're friendlier than the foals.

Be careful of the bee.

Go away!

It's angrier and faster than you, Toby!

3 Listen again and repeat. Act.

 Go to page 58

1 Look and say.

Let's learn!

Hooray. It's sunny today. It's sunn**ier than** yesterday.

Come on, it's dr**ier** in the barn **than** outside.

Jess is happ**ier than** Toby.

Take away *y* and add *ier*.
happy = happier   dry = drier

2 Write the sentences.

1 My sister's (happy) than my brother.

  My sister's happier than my brother.

2 Dad's (hungry) than Mum.

  _____

3 London's (cloudy) than Paris.

  _____

4 My teacher's (angry) than my mum.

  _____

3 Talk! Make sentences. Use the words in the box to help.

| sunny | noisy | happy | funny | tidy | cloudy | hungry |

A hen's noisier than a duckling.

It's sunnier today than yesterday.

Go to page 59

Vocabulary Presentation

1 Listen, point and repeat. 27

broken

fixed

open

closed

clean

shiny

noisy

washing machine

cloth

broom

2 Listen and read. 28

It was a good weekend. It was hot and sunny.

Not for me! Mum was angry because the washing machine was broken.

Dad was sad because the shop was closed.

Oh no!

I was kind and helpful.

Yes, the car is very clean and shiny!

3 Listen again and repeat. Act.

Go to page 60

1 Look and say.

Let's learn!

Yesterday

The window **was** open **because** it **was** hot and sunny.

Yesterday

The cloth **was** dry **because** it **was** in the sun.

Yesterday

You **were** angry **because** the brooms **were** broken.

We use **because** to connect sentences.

Singular object = was
Plural objects = were

2 Circle the correct words.

1 Mum **was** / were happy because the washing machine was fixed.

2 We **was** / **were** wet because the window was open.

3 Dad **was** / **were** angry because the kitchen was dirty.

4 You **was** / **were** comfortable because you were warm.

3 Talk! Make sentences with *because*. Use the words in the box to help.

| clean | noisy | kind | wet | bored | excited |

I was wet because it was raining.

Mum was angry because I was noisy.

Go to page 61

was / were   *because*   **Unit 14**   **29**

Vocabulary Presentation

1 Listen, point and repeat. 29

award

certificate

the winner

fifth

sixth

gold medal

silver medal

bronze medal

race

quiz

2 Listen and read. 30

This was our sports day.

Look, I was the winner of the race.

Were there any quizzes?

No, there weren't.

Were there any certificates?

I was fifth!

No. There were gold, silver and bronze medals.

How many people were there?

Five!

Toby's clever. He was second in the maths quiz today!

3 Listen again and repeat. Act.

Go to page 62

1 Look and say.

Were **there any** awards at the sports day?
No, there weren't. There were some medals.

How many medals **were there?**
There were three – gold, silver and bronze.

2 Circle the correct words.

1 Were there any skipping races? Yes, there **weren't** / **were**.

2 How many people were there in the race? **There were six.** / **Yes, there were.**

3 **Were there** / **There were** any gold medals?

4 How many awards **were there** / **there were**?

3 Talk! Point, ask and answer.

Yesterday

Were there any medals?

Yes, there were. How many people were in the race?

There were five people. Were there any men in the race?

No, there weren't.

Go to **63**

Were there any ...? How many ... were there? **Unit 15**

2nd Edition

Family and Friends Plus 2

Vocabulary and Grammar Practice

OXFORD

Jessica Finnis

Vocabulary Practice

1 Circle the correct word.

(1) ⟨paint pots⟩/
paint brushes

(2) rubber band /
string

(3) globe /
dictionary

(4) sink / easel

2 Write.

(1) e _a_ s _e_ l

(2) r _ _ be _
_ a n _ s

(3) g _ _ b _

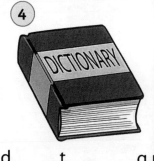
(4) d _ _ t _ _ _ a r

3 Write the word.

1 _globe_
2 _____
3 _____
4 _____
5 _____
6 _____

1 Circle the correct word.

1 **Are** / **Is** these our paint pots?

2 **Are** / **Is** this her globe?

3 **Is** / **Are** that your dictionary?

4 No, it **aren't** / **isn't**.

5 **Are** / **Is** those his rubber bands?

6 Yes, they **are** / **is**.

2 Write.

~~Are these~~   Are those   Is that   Is this

(1) ___Are these___ her paint pots?

(2) _____ his dictionary?

(3) _____ our rubber bands?

(4) _____ his easel?

3 Extended Practice Write.

isn't   aren't   ~~Is~~   those   paint pots   this

Jane ¹_____Is_____ this your dictionary?

Tom Yes, it is. Thank you. Is ²_____ your globe?

Jane No, it ³_____. It's Miss Percy's globe.

Tom Are ⁴_____ your paint pots?

Jane No, they ⁵_____. My ⁶_____ are in the sink.

They're happy now!

Vocabulary Practice

1 Find and circle the words.

doboredse

fifunnyin

wowetri

grlivelyor

2 Write.

e x _c_ _i_ _t_ e d

__ m b ___ ___ a s ___ d

___ ___ m f ___ t ___ l _

w ___ ___ m

3 Match.

wet

full

comfortable

dry

1 Look and write the opposites.

| tired | ~~bored~~ | dry | hungry |

1
He's bored.

2
_____

3
_____

4
_____

2 Write the answer.

1
Is she bored?
Yes, she is.

2
Is he cold?
_____

3
Is she wet?
_____

4
Are they lively?
_____

3 Extended Practice Read and number the pictures. Write sentences.

| ~~comfortable~~ | warm | wet | lively |

1 Tom's asleep on the sofa.   He's comfortable. _____

2 Jane and Debbie are outside in the rain. _____

3 Lucy runs in the park.   _____

4 I've got a hat, a scarf and a big coat. _____

Vocabulary Practice

1 Circle the correct words.

1	2	3	4
climb a mountain / ~~cross the road~~	build a sandcastle / ice skate	have a race / make a den	throw snowballs / climb a mountain

2 Write.

a   b   c   d

1 on top of   [d]
2 under   [ ]
3 opposite   [ ]
4 between   [ ]

3 Circle the incorrect word. Then write the sentences correctly.

1 I can ~~cross~~ a sandcastle.
   <u>I can build a sandcastle.</u>

2 You can have a den.
   _____

3 They can't build snowballs.
   _____

4 I can't throw the road.
   _____

1 **Write.**

1 <u>   Can you   </u> ice skate?   Yes, I can.

2 _____ make a den?   No, they can't.

3 _____ cross the road?   Yes, she can.

4 _____ climb a mountain?   No, he can't.

2 **Order the words.**

1 | can | very | throw snowballs | I | well. |

<u>   I can throw snowballs very well.   </u>

2 | climb mountains? | they | Can |

_____ ?

3 | well. | I | can | cross the road | quite |

_____

4 | build a sandcastle | They | well. | can | very |

_____

3 **Extended Practice** **Look and write.**   ✔✔ = very well   ✔ = quite well   ✗ = can't

Tom	✔✔		✗		
Lucy	✗				✔
Tom and Lucy		✔		✔✔	

Tom   <u>He can throw snowballs very well. He can't build a sandcastle.</u>

Lucy   _____

Tom and Lucy _____

Vocabulary Practice

1 Find and circle the words.

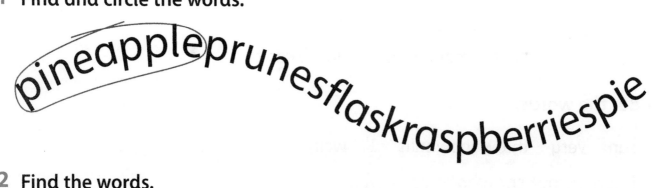

2 Find the words.

p	o	p	c	o	r	n	★	f	★
★	p	i	n	e	a	p	p	l	e
★	★	★	★	★	★	★	p	a	★
b	a	s	k	e	t	★	i	s	★
★	p	r	u	n	e	s	e	k	★

1 popcorn
2 pineapple
3 prunes
4 pie
5 flask
6 basket

3 Write.

s t r a w b e r r i e s

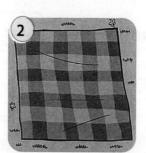

__ i __ n ___ b ___ ___ k ___

b a ___ ___ ___ t

b l ___ ___ ___ b ___ ___ ___ ___ s

1 Look and write.

popcorn   ~~pineapples~~   blackberries   strawberries

1   2   3   4

1 ('s got / some)   He's got some pineapples.

2 (haven't got / any)   _____

3 ('s got / some)   _____

4 (haven't got / any)   _____

2 Write the question. Use the word in brackets.

1 (they)   Have they got any flasks?

2 (he)   _____

3 (she)   _____

3 Extended Practice   **Write.**

've got   some   ~~Have you~~   haven't got   I have   any

Mum	¹ __Have you__ got any strawberries?
Shop keeper	Yes, ² _____.
Jane	Mum, he's got ³ _____ blackberries, but he hasn't got ⁴ _____ raspberries.
Shop keeper	I ⁵ _____ some raspberries here.
Mum	Oh no! I ⁶ _____ a basket.
Jane	Here you are, Mum.

We've got English!

Vocabulary Practice

1 Circle the correct word.

(1) history / science lab

(2) canteen / school gate

(3) head teacher / school bus

(4) woodwork / geography

2 Match.

 (1)

 (3)

 (5)

canteen

entrance

geography

school bus

science lab

workshop

(2)

(4)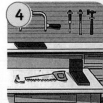

(6)

3 Look and write.

| canteen | ~~school gate~~ | woodwork | geography |

(1) school gate

(2) _____

(3) _____

(4) _____

1 Match.

1 Where have we got science? ☐ c   **a** In the classroom.
2 Where have we got lunch? ☐   **b** In the workshop.
3 Where have we got woodwork? ☐   **c** In the science lab.
4 Where have we got history? ☐   **d** In the canteen.

2 Circle the correct word to match the answer.

1 **(What)** / **When** / **Where** have we got every Monday?   We've got geography.
2 **What** / **When** / **Where** have you got woodwork?   In the workshop.
3 **What** / **When** / **Where** have we got woodwork?   On Thursday.
4 **What** / **When** / **Where** have we got science?   In the science lab.

3 [Extended Practice] Write.

| When | ~~What~~ | We've got | What | Where | workshop |

Will   Hi, Ben. ¹____What____ have we got this morning?

Ben   Hi, Will. ²_____ science.

Will   ³_____ have we got science?

Ben   In the science lab. Then we've got history in the classroom.

Will   ⁴_____ have you got after lunch?

Ben   I've got PE and a music lesson.

Will   I've got woodwork in the ⁵_____.

Ben   ⁶_____ have we got English?

Will   Tomorrow.

Vocabulary Practice

1 Circle the correct word.

go camping /
(go to the park)

paint a picture /
play the drums

go camping /
do homework

go for a walk /
watch a DVD

2 Write the sentences correctly.

I play the drums on Monday.

I go camping on Monday.

I go camping every Wednesday.

_____

I go to the park every Saturday.

_____

I do homework every night.

_____

3 Match.

1 We play ...   [b]   a to a café every morning.
2 She does sports ... [ ]   b the drums in music class.
3 I visit ...   [ ]   c in PE class.
4 He goes ...   [ ]   d friends every week.

1 Write. visit What ~~do~~ sports

1 What do you ____do____ after school on Monday?

2 I do _____. I play tennis and basketball.

3 Do you _____ your friends?

4 _____ do you do on weekends?

2 Tick (✔) the correct sentence. What do they do every Friday?

What do you do after
school every Friday?

John   Jane   Kate

John
a I play the drums. ✔
b I watch DVDs. ☐

Jane
a I go for a walk. ☐
b I go to a café. ☐

Kate
a I do homework. ☐
b I paint a picture. ☐

3 Extended Practice **Read and answer the questions.**

Dear Andy

Every Monday I do sports. I don't play the drums but my sister plays every Tuesday –
it's very noisy! Every Wednesday I go to the park with my mum and dad. On Saturday,
I visit friends and we watch DVDs. Every holiday I go camping with my family. It's fun.
What do you do after school?

From Bill

1 Does Bill do sports on Tuesday?   No, he doesn't. _____

2 When does Bill go to the park?   _____

3 What does Bill do on Saturday?   _____

4 Does Bill go camping on holiday?   _____

7 Let's buy presents!

Vocabulary Practice

1 Tick (✔) the correct sentence.

It's a paper plate. ✔
It's a napkin. ☐

It's a ribbon. ☐
It's jelly. ☐

It's a bouncy castle. ☐
It's wrapping paper. ☐

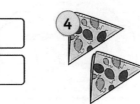
They're paper napkins. ☐
They're party bags. ☐

2 Find and circle the words.

robowerl

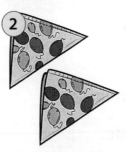
esnapkinset

gejellyin

ompartybagin

3 Write.

w r a p p i n g
p a p e r

r _ b _ _ _ n

_ l _ _ n

p _ _ _ _ y
_ a m _ _ _

1 Order the words.

1 | What | play? | to | does | like | he | _What does he like to play?_

2 | do | What | eat? | you | to | like | _____

3 | she | like | does | What | to | wear? | _____

4 | play? | What | like | you | do | to | _____

2 Look and write.

Jane		✔	✔	✔
Tom	✔			✔

1 What does Tom like to eat? _He likes to eat jelly._

2 What does Jane like to play? _____

3 What does Jane like to eat? _____

4 What do Tom and Jane like to do? _____

3 **Extended Practice** Write about you.

What do you like to eat? _I like to_ _____

What do you like to do on weekends? _____

What do you like to play? _____

What do you like to do at school? _____

What do you like to wear? _____

8 What's the time?

Vocabulary Practice

1 Match.

- wash my hair
- go downstairs
- wash my hands
- wake up
- have a dream
- go upstairs

2 Write.

go to sleep

3 Circle the correct words.

1 I **wake** / **have** / (**wash**) my hands every day.

2 I **get** / **have** / **go** a shower in the morning.

3 I **wake** / **has** / **get** dressed at 8 o'clock.

4 I **get** / **brush** / **have** a dream every night.

48 Unit 8 Everyday activities

1 Look and answer the questions.

 ①  ②  ③  ④

1 What time do you wake up?

   I wake up at 7 o'clock.

3 What time does she get dressed?

   _____ o'clock.

2 What time does he have a shower?

   _____ o'clock.

4 What time does he brush his teeth?

   _____ o'clock.

2 Order the words.

1 his teeth?　What　does　time　he　brush

_____

2 time　she　dressed?　get　does　What

_____

3 have　What　a shower?　you　time　do

_____

3 **Extended Practice** Complete the questions and the answers.

 ①

What time _____does_____ Jane ___wake up___?
She ___wakes up___ at ___8 o'clock___

 ②

What time _____ Simon _____?
He _____ at _____.

 ③

_____ Lucy _____?
She _____.

Where does she work?

1 Circle the correct word. Write.

It's a **market** /
petrol station.

It's a petrol
station.

It's a **post office** /
aquarium.

_____

_____

It's an
office block /
art gallery.

_____

_____

It's a
university /
campsite.

_____

_____

2 Write.

p _e_ t   sh _o_ p

a _ _ ar _ _ _ _

_ r _
g _ _ _ _ e _ y

t _ c _ _ _ _
o _ f _ _ e

3 Find and write the places.

1 postofficeartgallery   _post office_   _art gallery_

2 officeblockaquarium   _____   _____

3 petshopuniversity   _____   _____

4 campsitemarket   _____   _____

1 Circle the incorrect word. Then write the sentences correctly.

1 Where (does) you work?   <u>Where do you work?</u>

2 What time do he start work?   _____

3 Does you like your job?   _____

4 Where time do they start work? _____

2 Write. | What   like   do   ~~work~~   at   aquarium |

Peter Where do you ¹____work____?

Nancy I work at an ²_____.

Peter ³_____ time do you start work?

Nancy I start work ⁴_____ 9 o'clock.

Peter Do you ⁵_____ your job?

Nancy Yes, I ⁶_____.

3 [Extended Practice] **Look and write.**

1 She works in a <u>pet shop</u>. She starts work at <u>9 o'clock</u>.

2 They work in an _____. They start work at _____.

3 _____

4 _____

10 It's hot today!

1 Match.

1 stay … [b]   **a** a sun hat
2 use an … [ ]   **b** inside
3 wear … [ ]   **c** umbrella
4 go on … [ ]   **d** a boat

2 Write.

1 c _l_ _o_ u _d_ y

2 __ t a __
   i __ s i __ __

3 __ __ __ g __ y

4 r __ d __ a
   __ __ e __

3 Look and write. Find the mystery phrase.

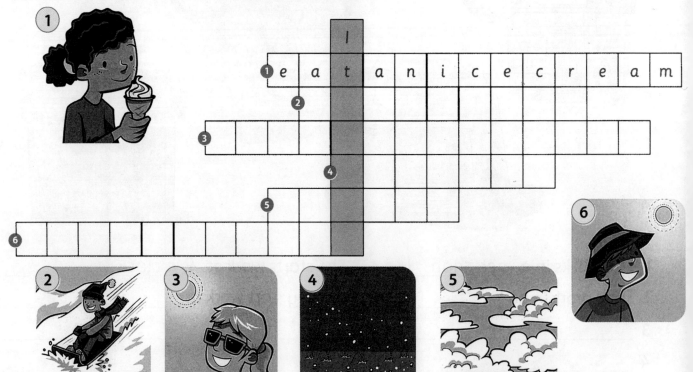

1 e a t   a n   i c e   c r e a m

1 Tick (✔) the correct sentence.

a It's hailing outside, so let's stay inside. ☐

b It's snowing this afternoon, so let's ride a sled. ✔

a It's foggy tonight, so let's watch DVDs. ☐

b It's raining outside, so let's use an umbrella. ☐

a It's hot today, so let's go on a boat. ☐

b It's cloudy today, so let's wear a coat. ☐

2 Write.

1 sunny / sun hat

It's sunny, so let's wear a sun hat.

3 foggy / sunglasses

_____

2 raining / umbrella

_____

4 warm / boat

_____

3 Extended Practice Read and answer.

1 Is it foggy on Monday?

No, it isn't. It's cloudy.

2 When is it hailing?

_____

3 Is it hot on Wednesday?

_____

4 What's the weather on Tuesday?

_____

Here's the weather forecast. On Monday, it's cloudy. On Tuesday it's foggy, so stay inside. On Wednesday it's hot, so wear sun hats. On Thursday and Friday, it's hailing.

Vocabulary Practice

1 Look and write.

1 ____suit____   2 _____   3 _____   4 _____

2 Circle the correct words.

 1   twenty to four /
(twenty past four)

 2   five to six /
five past seven

 3   twenty-five to
eleven / ten to eight

 4   twenty past twelve /
five past three

3 Tick (✔) the correct answer.

 1
    a It's five past three and he's wearing earmuffs. ☐
    b It's ten to six and he's wearing trainers. ☑

 2
    a It's twenty-five past nine and she's wearing a suit. ☐
    b It's twenty-five to nine and she's wearing a suit. ☐

 3
    a It's twenty to ten and he's wearing earmuffs. ☐
    b It's twenty to ten and he's wearing trainers. ☐

1 **Circle the correct words.**

1 What's **is eating** / **she wears** / (she eating)?

2 **Are she reading** / **Are they reading** / **Are they read** books?

3 What **is you watching** / **are you watching** / **does you watching**?

4 **Is she listening** / **Are she listening** / **Does she listening** to music?

2 **Write. Use the present continuous.**

1 He (listens) to music.   He's listening to music.

2 They (watch) Tom play football. _____

3 I (read) my history book. _____

4 You (eat) flatbread. _____

3 (Extended Practice) **Look and write.**

1 What's Grandpa looking at?   He's looking at a poster.

2 What's Jane wearing? _____

3 What are Tom and Grandma watching? _____

Write the questions.

4 _____?   She's eating an ice cream.

5 _____?   They're playing with a toy.

Vocabulary Practice

1 Write.

(1) m _a_ k _e_
a D _V_ _D_

(2) g _ _ o _ _ m

(3) l _ _ _ k
_ _ n _ _ h _ _
m _ _ _ _ _ r

(4) _ _ d d _ _ _ _
r i _ _ _

2 Order the letters.

(1) mogor
_____groom_____

(2) odvie mearca
_____

(3) treadoce
hte ekca
_____

(4) ebelctear
_____

3 Look and write.

1 d _ecorate the cake_ _____

2 m_____

3 b_____

4 l_____

5 w_____

6 m_____

1 Write.

1 What are the bridesmaids doing?   They're _looking_ in the mirror.

2 What's the groom doing?   He's _____ a speech.

3 What's the man doing?   He's _____ a DVD.

4 What's the woman doing?   She's _____ the cake.

2 Order the words.

1 | bride | the | What's | doing? | _What's the bride doing?_

2 | singing | She's | at | wedding. | the | _____

3 | doing? | parents | your | are | What | _____

4 | They're | cake. | the | eating | _____

3 Extended Practice **Write questions and answers.**

1 What's the bridesmaid doing?   _She's looking in the mirror._

2 What are the bride and groom doing?   _____

3 _____ ?   She's sleeping.

4 What's the boy doing?   _____

Write a question and answer.

_____ ?   _____

Vocabulary Practice

1 Circle the correct word.

(1)
calf / butterfly

(2)
corn / bee

(3)
lamb / foal

(4)
barn / tractor

2 Find and circle the words.

1 lambhentractor
3 calffoalbutterfly
5 ducklingsbeecorn

2 cornbeebarn
4 barnhenducklings
6 tractorhenfoal

3 Find the words.

d	u	c	k	l	i	n	g	s
c	★	★	★	a	★	c	★	★
a	★	b	★	m	★	o	★	★
l	★	e	★	b	a	r	n	h
f	★	e	★	★	★	n	★	e
★	t	r	a	c	t	o	r	n
b	u	t	t	e	r	f	l	y
★	f	o	a	l	★	★	★	★

1 tractor	2 ducklings
3 bee	4 lamb
5 butterfly	6 foal
7 hen	8 calf
9 barn	10 corn

1 Write the sentences.

1 Jane / friendly / Tom

   Jane's friendlier than Tom.

3 bathroom / tidy / bedroom

   _____

2 drums / noisy / guitars

   _____

4 ducklings / happy / hens

   _____

2 Write the sentences.

 The girl's happy. The boy isn't happy.

   The girl's happier than the boy.

 The lamb's friendly. The foal isn't friendly.

   _____

 Egypt's sunny. England isn't sunny.

   _____

3 **Extended Practice** **Compare the pictures.** | sunny ~~friendly~~ noisy tidy |

New Town

Old Town

1 _The boy's friendlier than the girl._____

2 New Town's _____

3 _____

4 _____

Look at the photos!

1 Match.

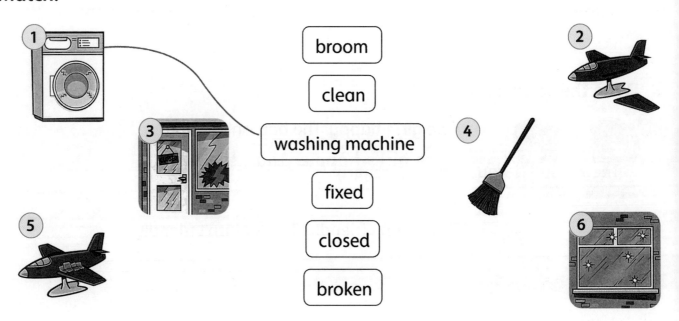

broom

clean

washing machine

fixed

closed

broken

2 Write.

s <u>h</u> i n y   n _ _ _ y   _ _ _ _ t h   o _ _ e _

3 Write.   open   closed   ~~clean~~   noisy

1 I was happy because my room was ___clean___.

2 They were angry because the boy was _____.

3 The park was _____ because it was raining.

4 They were excited because the shop was _____.

1 **Match.**

1 I wasn't good at football yesterday … [c]   **a** because they were warm.
2 They were comfortable … [   ]   **b** because you were sick.
3 They weren't happy outside … [   ]   **c** because I was tired.
4 You weren't at school yesterday … [   ]   **d** because it was foggy.

2 **Write the sentences. Use *was* / *were*.**

1 I'm at the park because it's sunny.

  <u>I was at the park because it was sunny.</u>

2 They're sad because they're hungry.

  _____

3 You're cold because you're wet.

  _____

3 **Extended Practice** **Complete the sentences.**

① The window was open <u>because it was hot</u>.

② They weren't happy because _____.

③ She was angry _____.

④ _____.

Vocabulary Practice

1 Circle the correct words.

1. (sixth) / fifth
2. award / gold medal
3. quiz / bronze medal
4. race / certificate

2 Look and write.

1. fifth
2. _____
3. _____
4. _____

3 Look and write.

1 r ace _____

2 a _____

3 s _____

4 w _____

5 g _____

6 b _____

1 Write.

1 Were there any gold medals?

No, there weren't.

2 Were there any bronze medals?

_____

3 How many certificates were there?

_____

4 _____?

Yes, there were.

2 Order the words.

1 Were | winners? | any | there

Were there any winners?

2 many | How | awards | there? | were

_____

3 yesterday? | any | Were | races | there

_____

4 How | there? | certificates | were | many

_____

3 **Extended Practice** Read and answer.

Sports Day!

Yesterday the pupils were very excited because it was Sports Day. There were three races. Jane was the winner of two medals for skipping and running. The teachers were in a running race and Miss Smith was fifth! There were a lot of happy parents.

1 Was there a skipping race?

Yes, there was.

2 How many races were there?

_____

3 Were the parents sad?

_____

4 Was Miss Smith sixth in the running race?

_____

5 Was Jane the winner of the skipping race?

_____

Grammar reference

Unit 1   *this / these / that / those*

	questions	short answers
	Is this your tape?	**Yes, it is. / No, it isn't.**
	Are these his paint brushes?	**Yes, they are. / No, they aren't.**
	Is that her dictionary?	**Yes, it is. / No, it isn't.**
	Are those their paint pots?	**Yes, they are. / No, they aren't.**

Unit 2   Adjectives

affirmative
I'm bored.
You're funny.
He's lively.
She's brave.
We're excited.
They're embarrassed.

opposites
bored – excited
hungry – full
wet – dry
cold – hot
lively – tired
happy – sad

questions	short answers
Are you comfortable?	**Yes, I am. / No, I'm not.**
Is he full?	**Yes, he is. / No, he isn't.**
Is she funny?	**Yes, she is. / No, she isn't.**
Are they wet?	**Yes, they are. / No, they aren't.**

Unit 3 *can / can't*

affirmative	negative
I can climb a mountain.	**I can't** ice skate.
You can throw snowballs.	**You can't** play tennis.
He / She can build a sandcastle.	**He / She can't** make a den.
We can cross the road.	**We can't** ride horses.
They can have a race.	**They can't** climb a mountain.

Use extra words to describe how well someone can or can't do something.

I can throw snowballs **quite** well.	✔
She can throw snowballs **very** well.	✔✔

questions	short answers
Can you cross the road?	**Yes, I can. / No, I can't.**

Unit 4 *have got (some / any)*

affirmative	negative
I've got some raspberries.	**I haven't got any** cheese.
You've got some prunes.	**You haven't got any** fries.
He's got some blackberries.	**He hasn't got any** raspberries.
She's got some cheese.	**She hasn't got any** prunes.
We've got some fries.	**We haven't got any** strawberries.
They're got some strawberries.	**They haven't got any** blackberries.

	questions	short answers
	Have you got any raspberries?	**Yes, I have. / No, I haven't.**

Unit 5   *Where / What / When*

	questions	answers
	Where have you got geography**?**	**I've got** geography in the classroom.
	What have we got after lunch**?**	**We've got** history.
	When have we got woodwork**?**	**We've got** woodwork on Monday.

Unit 6   Questions with long and short answers

questions	answers
What do you do after school on Wednesday**?**	I do my homework.
Do you visit friends after school**?**	**Yes, I do. / No, I don't.**

Unit 7   *What do you like* + verb

questions	answers
What do you like **to play?**	I like **to play** party games.
What do you like **to eat?**	I like **to eat** jelly.
What do you like **to watch?**	I like **to watch** films.
What do you like **to wear?**	I like **to wear** trousers.
What do you like **to do?**	I like **to** draw and read.

Unit 8   *What time ...?*

	questions	answers
	What time do you brush your teeth?	**I** brush my teeth **at 7 o'clock.**
	What time does he go to sleep?	**He** goes to sleep **at 9 o'clock.**

Unit 9   Questions with *do*

questions	answers
Where do you work?	I work at a pet shop.
What time do you finish work?	I finish work at 5 o'clock.
Do you like your job?	Yes, I do.

Unit 10   Weather questions

	questions	answers
	Is it cloudy today?	**Yes, it is. / No, it isn't.**

so let's ...

	Affirmative
	It's foggy today, **so let's** stay inside.
	It's hailing, **so let's** use an umbrella.

Unit 11 Present continuous questions

questions	short answers
Are you wear**ing** earmuffs?	**Yes, I am. / No, I'm not.**
Is she watch**ing** a film?	**Yes, she is. / No, she isn't.**
Are they eat**ing** strawberries?	**Yes, they are. / No they aren't.**

questions	answers
What **are** you read**ing**?	I**'m** read**ing** a magazine.
What**'s** she watch**ing**?	She**'s** watch**ing** a DVD.
What **are** they eat**ing**?	They**'re** eat**ing** popcorn.
What**'s** he listen**ing** to?	He**'s** listen**ing** to music.

Unit 12 Present continuous with the verb *to do*

questions	answers
What**'s the** groom do**ing**?	**He's** look**ing** in the mirror.
What **are the** bridesmaids do**ing**?	**They're** danc**ing**.
What**'s your** mum do**ing**?	**She's** decorat**ing** a cake.
What **are your** brothers do**ing**?	**They're** mak**ing** a DVD.

Unit 13 Comparatives (adjectives ending in -*y*)

affirmative statement	comparative statement
A tractor's nois**y**.	A tractor's nois**ier than** a car.
Summer's sunn**y**.	Summer's sunn**ier than** winter.
I'm hungr**y**.	I'm hungr**ier than** you.
The bee's angr**y**.	The bee's angr**ier than** the butterfly.

Unit 14 Past simple + *because*

affirmative		
I **was** excited …	because	it **was** the weekend.
The man **was** happy …	because	the shop **was** open.
She **was** sad …	because	her toy **was** broken.
We **were** comfortable …	because	we **were** inside.
They **were** outside …	because	it **was** sunny.

Unit 15 Past simple questions

	questions	short answers
	Were there any races yesterday?	**Yes, there were. /** **No, there weren't.**
	Were there any winners in the quiz?	**Yes, there were. /** **No, there weren't.**

	questions	answers
	How many medals **were there?**	**There were** three.

Wordlist

Unit 1
dictionary
easel
globe
paint brushes
paint pots
rubber bands
sink
string
tape
whiteboard

Unit 2
bored
comfortable
dry
embarrassed
excited
full
funny
lively
warm
wet

Unit 3
build a sandcastle
climb a mountain
cross the road
have a race
ice skate
make a den
on top of
opposite
throw snowballs
under

Unit 4
basket
blackberries
flask
picnic blanket
pie
pineapple
popcorn
prunes
raspberries
strawberries

Unit 5
canteen
entrance
geography
head teacher
history
school bus
school gate
science lab
woodwork
workshop

Unit 6
do homework
do sports
go camping
go for a walk
go to a café
go to the park
paint a picture
play the drums
visit friends
watch a DVD

Unit 7
bouncy castle
bow
clown
jelly
napkins
paper plate
party bag
party games
ribbon
wrapping paper

Unit 8
brush my teeth
have a dream
have a shower
get dressed
go downstairs
go to sleep
go upstairs
wake up
wash my hair
wash my hands

Unit 9
aquarium
art gallery
campsite
market
office block
pet shop
petrol station
post office
ticket office
university

Unit 10
cloudy
eat an ice cream
foggy
go on a boat
hailing
ride a sled
stay inside
use an umbrella
wear a sun hat
wear sunglasses

Unit 11
earmuffs
five past
nightdress
pyjamas
suit
ten to
trainers
twenty past
twenty-five past
twenty-five to

Unit 12
bridesmaids
celebrate
decorate the cake
groom
look in the mirror
make a DVD
make a speech
video camera
wedding dress
wedding ring

Unit 13
barn
bee
butterfly
calf
corn
ducklings
foal
hen
lamb
tractor

Unit 14
broken
broom
clean
closed
cloth
fixed
noisy
open
shiny
washing machine

Unit 15
award
bronze medal
certificate
fifth
gold medal
quiz
race
silver medal
sixth
the winner

Great Clarendon Street, Oxford, OX2 6DP, United Kingdom

Oxford University Press is a department of the University of Oxford.
It furthers the University's objective of excellence in research, scholarship,
and education by publishing worldwide. Oxford is a registered trade
mark of Oxford University Press in the UK and in certain other countries

ISBN: 978 0 19 440343 6

Printed in China

This book is printed on paper from certified and well-managed sources

ACKNOWLEDGEMENTS

Illustrations by: Andrew Hamilton pp.2 (top), 3, 4 (top), 6 (top), 8 (top), 10 (top),
12 (top), 14 (top), 16 (top), 18 (top), 20 (top), 22 (top), 24 (top), 26 (top), 28 (top),
30 (top), 32 (top), 34 (top), 36 (top), 37 (top), 38 (top), 39, 40, 42, 44, 46, 47, 48,
50, 52, 53, 54, 56, 58, 60, 62 (top), 64, 65, 66, 67, 69; Dušan Pavlić/Beehive
pp.2 (bottom), 3 (top), 4 (bottom), 5 (top), 6 (bottom), 7 (top), 8 (bottom), 9,
10 (bottom), 11 (top), 12 (bottom), 13 (top), 14 (bottom), 15, 16 (bottom), 17,
18 (bottom), 19, 20 (bottom), 21 (top), 22 (bottom), 23 (top), 24 (bottom),
25 (top), 26 (bottom), 27, 28 (bottom), 29, 30 (bottom), 31 (top); Matt Ward/
Beehive pp.5 (bottom), 7 (bottom), 11 (bottom), 13 (bottom), 21 (middle),
23 (bottom), 25 (middle), 31 (bottom), 34 (bottom), 35, 37 (bottom), 38 (middle),
41, 43, 45, 49, 51, 53 (bottom), 54 (middle, bottom), 55, 56 (bottom), 57, 59, 61,
62 (bottom), 63.